The

Beginning a Lifestyle of Prayer

An Average Person/Housewife Learning How to Reach Heaven Through Prayer

By Chevelle L. Tigner-Moore

PUBLISH AMERICA

PublishAmerica
Baltimore

First printing

PublishAmerica has allowed this work to remain exactly as the author intended, verbatim, without editorial input.

ISBN: 1-60474-907-5
PUBLISHED BY PUBLISHAMERICA, LLLP
www.publishamerica.com
Baltimore

Printed in the United States of America

Dedication

This book is dedicated to my mother, Delilah Owens-LaGrone, who went home to be with the Lord on Easter Sunday, 4/11/2004, her favorite holiday; and of course my Papa, John Franklin Owens.

Acknowledgments

First I would like to give honor to God, the only real father I've ever known; to my savior, the Lord Jesus Christ, who set me free and plays a major role in my life helping me never to give up; and of course the Precious Holy Spirit, who is so faithful to comfort me and lead me while on my journey. To my dear husband Kenneth, who has been an encouragement to me and reminds me of the victories in my hard times and how much God has used me in prayer and intercession for others. To my dear children David, Phillip and Kemar, who are my constant reminder of the joy that a lifestyle of prayer can bring.

Let us pray: Dear heavenly Father, I come to You today first asking, Father, that You bless me as I read this book. I ask that the Holy Spirit will take away any of my doubts and fears that may exist that I'm not aware of concerning my personal prayer life. Father, I pray that You will cause a spirit of obedience to rise up in my spirit with holy boldness to declare I am free to pray the heart of God for my life and others around me. Father, I pray that a spirit of authority will rise up in me as never before to crush the head of the enemy/devil in my life and the lives of those I pray for, in Jesus' Mighty Name—AMEN!

I would like to start off by saying thank-you to those who support me by reading this book. This was a big step for me, and I hope and pray it will be a blessing to you and others in your sphere of influence.

Well, let's get started!

The Basics of Beginning a Lifestyle of Prayer

An Average Person/Housewife Learning How to Reach Heaven Through Prayer

Introduction

I was coming from Bible study one day when Sue, the lady with whom I was carpooling, started saying she just didn't know how to get started in a life of prayer. I offered my assistance by telling her I'm available (if you know me), and that I had taught on prayer before. You see, I had just returned from a N.W. intercessors' conference in Portland, Oregon, and I was on fire, bubbling inside to share anything about prayer to anyone, anywhere, who would listen! She said, "I can tell by the way you pray at the Bible study." Well, I hadn't paid any attention to the fact of anyone noticing me.

The Holy Spirit had now taken over the conversation for us by having her ask questions like, "When do you pray? How do you pray? Why do you pray?" I answered all her questions and she seemed to be content with my answers. As I was getting ready to get out of the car, the Lord impressed my heart to ask if I could pray for her. She said yes, and I did.

You see, it has always been a burden in my heart for people around me to be able to be free in their personal prayer life. By free, I mean just that—FREEDOM (LIBERTY). Now the Lord is that spirit; and where the spirit of the Lord is, there is Liberty. 2nd Corinthians 3:17 kjv.

It has been a mission for years for me to help others get a breakthrough in starting and keeping a consistent life of prayer. I know first-hand how it can be overwhelming at times and how the enemy/devil fights us before we even getting started. That is why I'm writing this book and sharing my testimony on how I got started. I truly believe it will bless you mightily.

Chapter One
Seeds Need to Be Planted

I was raised being sent to church with my only brother Richard, whom I love dearly. My mom hardly ever went to church except for holidays and special occasions, but she was sure faithful to send us (thanks, Mom). I mostly went to church with my Grandpa, whom we called Papa. His name was John Franklin Owens, the greatest man that ever walked the earth outside of Jesus Christ (in my eyes, of course).

I believe he played a major role in my life where prayer was concerned. He was the only person I saw praying outside of church services. He would also tell me to watch what I prayed for. My papa would take time to share with me different stories about answered prayers he had received, and answered prayers he didn't want to receive.

This influenced me mightily as a little girl. I mean, I literally prayed about everything. I prayed for my dogs, my family, I mean everything. I mean, for a little girl, I had a very good prayer life, wouldn't you say so? Even when I had eaten all my candy, I would pray that the Lord would fill my wrappers back up before morning so I would have some for the next day. You see, my brother and I were only allowed to buy candy once a month and when it was gone, it was gone, and I had to wait until the next month to receive more. So you see, I had an obligation to pray. Well, as you probably know, my wrappers were never filled back up, but you can truly believe each and every month when those wrappers were empty again, little Chevelle would pray, "God, please fill my wrappers back up." Sometimes I would pray all night. This went on for a long time. After all, he answered most of my other prayers, why not this one? I was not giving up! I guess that's where my persistence came from—all that practice I had with those wrappers. Go ahead, you can laugh. I still do to this day when I share this story.

I've shared all this to say that there has to be a seed planted on prayer so that it can bring forth fruition in our prayer lives. However, if you choose to believe my stories in this book, even though they may seem silly or foolish, 1st Corinthians 1:27 says, but God has chosen the foolish things of the world to put to shame the wise, and God has chosen the weak things of the world to put to shame the things which are mighty (NKJ). God will allow my testimony to plant a seed in your life or water a seed that has already been planted so he can bring the increase. In 1st Corinthians 3:7, it says—then neither he who plants is anything, nor he who waters, but God who gives the increase (NKJ). We have to be the ones to choose to believe. He will not force it upon us. We are free-willed and he is not a God to force anything upon us. If you haven't had a seed planted yet, let me share something. It's never too late with God, and if you're just starting or if you've been praying for a while, I truly hope you will allow this book to touch your life the way God has ordered your steps for Him, too.

Chapter Two

Adulthood—Getting Started

I'm going to move ahead to my adulthood, the part where I determined in my heart to get reborn and that I would never leave the Lord again. I was ready for whatever God wanted to do to me and through me. In other words, I was sick and tired of being sick and tired (that's another book within itself). I was ready to find the key that keeps us connected to God the Father.

Well, here's my testimony. I was a member of King of Glory Church. I had been away from the Lord for a while. This church had what we called a mother's board. For those of you who were allowed to skip the church of tradition (lol) a mother's board consists of the elderly women who oversee the church with prayer, especially keeping the young women of faith on a sanctified path with being an example of how to dress, etc.

One day I was speaking with a mother who always said to me, "You have such a sweet spirit, my dear. You just keep serving the Lord with all your heart." Every time she would say that to me, it would give me some hope, but when I went home, my house was in shambles.

The enemy/devil would keep my house in an uproar. My husband and I didn't see eye to eye on anything, let alone spiritual things like prayer. I truly thank God for the scripture Ephesians 6:12—for we do not wrestle with flesh and blood, but against principalities, against powers, against the rulers of the darkness of this age, against spiritual hosts of wickedness in the heavenly places (NKJ). This scripture kept me during the rough times when I was trying to establish an intimate relationship with God through prayer.

Please don't misunderstand me; it keeps me now too. (I know I haven't arrived yet. I'm still a work in progress.)

I'm also not saying by any means that my husband did not love the Lord; it's just that he had a lot of issues he was dealing with in his renewed salvation.

One day after service, one of the mothers and I were sitting on the pews and I felt this desperate boldness rise up in me to ask her, "How do I keep serving the Lord when my home is in shambles?"

She told me to start a prayer closet by praying for an hour every day and things would begin to change for me. You have to know she had to explain prayer closet to me. I was just a babe in the Lord at that time. I literally thought I had to go into my clothes closet and pray (it was not that big). I asked her, "What do you mean by prayer closet?"

She said, "Honey, you don't have to get in your clothes closet." (I thought to myself, *Thank goodness, I might suffocate.*) She said that I did have to go in a private place and spend time with God in prayer at least one hour a day. She used the story in the scriptures about when Jesus went to the Garden of Gethsemane with the disciples and asked them to pray, but they fell fast asleep. He said to Peter, "What! Could you not watch with me one hour? Watch and pray, lest you enter into temptation. The spirit is willing, but he flesh is weak. Again a second time He went to pray and he came and found them asleep again for their eyes were heavy. So He left them went away to pray again the third time. When He came back again He asked them Are you still sleeping and resting?" (You pretty much know the ending of that story.) Because of the story I took the mother literally about praying for an hour. I believed and still do believe that if they were watching and praying, the enemy would not have been able to sneak up on them and they would have been aware of what was about to happen. Yes, I do know the scriptures had to be fulfilled but this had just become so very clear to me. I'm not saying you have to pray an hour every time you enter into your personal time with God. No, not by any means. My suggestion is to start with a prayer time you're comfortable with.

It could even be three minutes—just do your best and do your best to increase it every time you enter into your personal prayer time when you're starting out. Really try to stay the same or increase, never decrease, your time when starting out so that God can stretch your spiritual praying muscles. This will also make your prayer foundation strong. You'll find in doing this that the more time you spend with God, the more He will release his presence and fill you with the anointing that can destroy the bondages and yoke that keep us hindered in our everyday lives. There is nothing like the anointing of God being released in our lives.

There's an old saying that goes like this: NO prayer NO power SOME prayer SOME power MUCH prayer MUCH power. I'm sure by now you get the point. I do apologize for driving that nail on the head so hard, but I sincerely want you to get everything God has for you. From my testimony, you see I was just a normal housewife raising kids, trying to further my education and be the first one in my family to STAY married. One day I looked up to heaven and cried out to God for help. He heard my cry, picked me up, turned me around, and placed my feet on solid praying ground. AMEN.

Chapter Three
Get Ready, Set, Go!

I began to go into my bedroom for prayer one full hour every day. As I look back I tried to help my husband and my only sister Regeine with their prayer lives by taking them into my prayer closet, but after ten or fifteen minutes, I'd look up and they'd be gone. They thought I was nuts. (I'm sure they don't think that now—ha!) I learned taking people into your own personal prayer time WILL NOT WORK. For one, it distracts and can cause a quenching of the flow of the Holy Spirit. Let's move on. After a season of disciplining myself in prayer, the Lord blessed me by teaching me through an awesome woman of God named Ignitia. She taught me about being awakened by the Holy Spirit to pray in the middle of the night. She first gave me her testimony. (I chose to believe her and trust God; that is why it worked for me.) She taught me that if I started tossing and turning at night and couldn't go back to sleep, it was because the Lord was wooing me to prayer. The first time I tried it, I got up in the middle of the night. I went into my living room while my husband and my three sons were fast asleep and I began to pray. As I began, I felt this fear come upon me so strong that I turned on the light and then I began to pray again, not really knowing what I was going to pray about. I just started tarrying like the mothers in the church would tell you to do when you're trying to get filled with the Holy Ghost with the evidence of speaking in tongues. They used to tell us to just keep saying, "Thank you, Jesus; thank you, Jesus; I love you, Jesus," over and over and praise Him. He will infill you.

I began to say this and right then, all of a sudden, I heard this extremely loud noise of a slamming door; of course it startled me. I thought it was my husband who slammed the door because he didn't want to hear me praying so I got up and went down my hallway to check it out. Well, none of the doors were closed. As a matter of fact, they were wide open. In my room I found my husband sound asleep. In my sons' room they were sound asleep as well. I was in shock. I couldn't believe my eyes. So I went back in the living room and continued to pray.

The next time I saw Ignitia at church I told her of the event that had happened. She said something just like this: "Girl, that was the enemy/devil trying to put fear in you so you wouldn't pray, that's all. If it happens again, Chevelle, just rebuke him in the name of Jesus!" Rebuking means:

to force back; a sharp reprimand (*Webster's* definition). With me being a babe in the Lord. she explained it to me like this: Rebuking is the authority we have to overcome the enemy/devil. She said, "Do this until he flees; don't let him intimidate you. Girl, he's a defeated foe!" Well, let me warn you, when you tell a zealous/hungry/tired of being sick and tired babe in the Lord who's seeking the Lord this, she/he takes what you say just as it is. There is this scripture that helped me—we walk by faith and not by sight—2nd Corinthians 5:7 —hat became so real to me. I also would like to say the scripture in 2nd Timothy 1:7—for God has not given us a spirit of fear but of power love and a sound mind—became even more real to me as well. With that being said I would like to expound a little more by saying I will never forget that experience ever. I found out first-hand that we can't go by what we hear or even by what we see. The enemy/devil is waiting to put something in our path of vision/hearing to put fear and doubt in us no matter what level we are in God, but especially a babe. Another thing is that the enemy/devil's little wicked snares will always try to come in when we are seeking more of God. We have to remember to get the scriptures written on the tablets of our hearts NO MATTER WHAT, pressing our way NO MATTER WHAT and asking God to help us to remember NO MATTER WHAT! He is so faithful and just. He will do just that—IF—we just believe.

Just remember NO MATTER WHAT level we are in, we are NOTHING without HIM!

I would like to share some more examples of resisting/rebuking the enemy/devil in the scriptures, but before I do, I bet some of you are saying, "Why is she making the enemy/devil's name in such small lettering?" Well, I'm doing this to remind my readers that we have and serve a great BIG GOD and are opposed by a little bitty devil. We just can't be foolish and act like he does not exist. Okay, with that being said, here are the scriptures: James 4:7, Mark 4:39, Mark 8:33. I encourage you to look them up and BELIEVE!

Allow me to share the main scripture that has helped me and many other people (I've witnessed) to overcome fear. It is 2nd Timothy 1:7. This is a scripture you definitely want written on the tablet of your heart no matter what level you're on; it will keep you grounded in knowing the authority you have in Christ Jesus and who He is in you! Another thing I want to share is that we need to keep ourselves cleansed from sin. Be quick to repent and remember to ask God to GIVE you a repentant heart. With this remember that we not only fight against our flesh to get back up from falling down and a need to repent, we also have the enemy/devil riding our coattails to make us feel like we canNOT pray and canNOT get back up, but in reality all God is looking for is a repentant HEART. God is so good that we never ever have to start our salvation walk from the beginning because God does not condemn. We can get an awesome fresh start right from where we left off, praying just as strong, being loved by him just as much! God does REALLY cast all of our sins into the sea of forgetfulness. We just have to remember to forgive ourselves. Tip—

pray that the Holy Spirit (even if you're not spirit-filled evidence of speaking in tongues because remember, you are a new creature in Christ, no longer bound by sin) 2nd Corinthians 5:17 (paraphrased). This will help you to be aware of the sin in your life because sometimes we sin in our thoughts and deeds as well.

Always remember the enemy/devil is looking for a way to block us from our authority in God through Christ Jesus, and of course that is what prayer does—it gives us AUTHORITY.

Okay, let's return to the part of my testimony on having to receive people for who they are.

So I did as Ignitia instructed me to do. As I look back, I realize that if I hadn't stepped out in faith by listening to her, the vessel that God chose to send to me, I would not have gone to the next level in Him. I would not have received growth in that season. God is merciful and faithful and would have sent someone else another time, but me being a desperate housewife and mother, and sick and tired of being sick and tired, by receiving her, I did not have to wait.

I feel the need to share this with you all as well. In my year of personal prayer training by the Holy Spirit and receiving those who were sent to me to water seeds that was planted in my life as a child by my papa, I did not find myself attracted to them to be their friends. I'll be honest: I would have never had a relationship with them if it weren't for almighty God and my hunger for more of Him.

There are three lessons you can learn from this:

#1—It's not just a vessel (person) you are receiving alone. We have to be open to Him for whoever He decides to send to us. It's Jesus Christ in them. We can't afford spiritually to be picky about who He sends to us. We have to be open to Him for whoever he decides to send us. That's where that walking by faith and not by sight kicks in even more! Warning: He can send anyone! I'm not exaggerating. (Boy, do I have some stories.)

#2—This lesson is straight scripture (logos—written word) "...as we draw nigh to God, He draws nigh to us. Cleanse your hands, ye sinners; and purify your hearts ye double minded." James 4:8 KJV. This scripture is commanding us to stop allowing the old way of thinking to rule our minds and allow the new way to come upon us, by believing His word for what it says and allowing it to become more real to us than ever so we can be changed for His Glory (let it become Rhema). It is to purify our hearts and cleanse our hands and also to cease double-mindedness in our lives. By drawing nigh to Him, we can't help but be changed for the better by becoming more like Him and less like the person we were before giving our lives to Jesus. Therefore if any man be in Christ Jesus, He is a new creature; old things are passed away and behold, all things are become new. 2nd Corinthians 5:17 NKJ.

#3—Never worry about understanding completely the word of God. The most important thing is that you read it! It's just like feeding our natural bodies food. We never fully remember what we ate the day before yesterday or even yesterday, for that matter. All we really remember is that we ate to nurture our bodies in order to stay alive and have physical strength. Well, that's just how reading the word is for our spirit. It feeds our spirit and soul for change and strength as we allow. Always keep in mind God will bring the revelation in His timing for our growth (the increase).

JUST A TIP (for free)—When trying to memorize a verse, read it, write it, and quote it over and over again. I even went as far as putting them on my walls by the mirror in the bathroom, my children's wall in their room, by my bed, etc.

Chapter Four
Setting Our Boundaries

While looking back in starting out with my personal prayer life, I had to put my foot down with my kids and my husband about not disturbing me when I'm in prayer. This was mainly because I had not yet started making God my first priority in my day. I had started praying every day, but not first in my day. It was summer and the kids were home all day. That meant that they would need all my attention no matter what. They would knock on my door while I was in prayer. As a beginner, this would totally throw me off track. I had to grow up being a mother and especially a spiritual mother—there's a big difference. Since they had not been introduced to the Lord just yet, I had to give them something to do and tell them unless it was an absolute emergency, they must not knock on my door because I was spending time with Jesus. I don't know if they completely understood the "spending time with Jesus" part, but they understood the "do not disturb mamma" part. That's all that really mattered at that time in our lives. I had to teach them about respecting the Lord and me too, but especially if someone was praying, that meant that they were trying to spend time with Jesus and it was rude to interrupt. It was very important for me at that time, because I was just starting out. The poor kids were so used to getting my attention anytime and whenever they wanted it. They did adjust, though. They actually grew up knowing Jesus very well. When my husband Kenneth was at home with his friend the T.V, I had to remind him to not to let the kids disturb me and that he couldn't disturb me either. He had to be Mom and Dad for that hour. If you'll notice, my family was my life. This order went on until I learned what the word says. "But seek ye first the kingdom of God and his righteousness, and all things shall be added unto you." Mathew 6:33. Once I took that word and allowed God to make it real to me I started going after God in a whole new way and a new time. (Boy, the enemy was mad.) As for me, I didn't care. I was falling more and more in love with Jesus and who He is while learning who God really is and who my new friend, the Holy Spirit, is. So I kept right on praying. I even went as far as finding me a phone prayer partner, and of course it was the very same lady Ignitia. I knew in my spirit she had the keys I needed to open the heavens in my life. Ignitia is the one God used to teach me about the scripture. Ignitia was so very much used by God to help me form a solid foundation in my faith concerning prayer as an adult. I will never forget her. I thank God for her obedience. We started spending time on the phone in the evenings praying for different personal needs that each other had and for church and of course our pastor. I was beginning to graduate into an intercessor (that's another book). This is what got me started in my love for prayer and knowledge of how important prayer can be. Yes, some warfare still comes and goes, but staying in God's presence behind the veil helps us not to feel the storm of the warfare around us. God is so faithful to put people in our paths to help us along the way from faith to faith and from level to level. I pray that you will just keep pressing toward the high calling of God through Christ Jesus. Philippians 3:14 KJV says, "…and he will meet you right where you are ALWAYS." We've asked Jesus Christ as our Lord and Savior. For those of you who have not accepted Jesus Christ as your personal Lord and Savior, I encourage you to do so with me right now. In the book of Romans, Chapter 10, Verses 9 and 10, it says that "if thou shalt confess with thy mouth the Lord Jesus, and shalt believeth unto righteousness; and with the mouth confession is made unto salvation." Let's pray together:

Dear Heavenly Father, I come before you now confessing that I want your son Jesus Christ to come into my heart as my personal Lord and Savior. I do believe that You sent him to die on the cross just for me and that He rose again in three days. I renounce all my sins and want to turn from my wicked ways to walk with You from this day forward. IN Jesus' precious name, I pray. Amen! (Angels are rejoicing in heaven on your behalf.)

I am a firm believer that it's better to know beyond a shadow of doubt that you are saved by grace than to spend the rest of your life guessing.

Some of you may have already been dedicated to the Lord, but it's far better to make sure we all are in the kingdom and have received the eternal gift of life. It's also so much better to close all doors to the enemy/devil so that we can prosper in the spirit and please our heavenly Father. When our ways please Him, even our enemies are at peace with us. Proverbs 16:7 KJV. Isn't it good He covers all the bases that need covering in our lives? He closes all the doors the enemy/devil may have opened. He opens all the doors the enemy/devil may have closed in our lives as well. He also makes sure that He is the door opener and closer from that day forward if we'll let Him. HALLELUJAH!

Chapter Five

Becoming More Disciplined in Prayer

Now your experience may be different than mine when beginning a lifestyle of prayer. I mean the kind of a lifestyle of prayer that keeps you even when you're going through a very hard time or even on the verge of throwing in the towel while thinking to yourself, *I don't care if I'm kept.* You must know no matter who you are, that it takes perseverance, discipline and dedication to receive from God a good solid foundational lifestyle of prayer. The scriptures provided in this book will help you tremendously as you quote them and use them daily. They will give you strength and assurance of who you are in Christ Jesus and who He is in you.

Side note: If you have noticed, I used all King James Version and none of the awesome versions of the Bible that's available to us now. The reason for doing this is that KJV helped me so much while getting the foundation of the scriptures written on the tablets of my heart. I believe the Holy Spirit caused the word to stick to my memory and my heart. I have tried and tried to memorize the other versions of the Bible but it just does not work for me. You use what ever version you're comfortable with. I advise to use the KJV; it's just something about that version that has really been used in my life and my children's lives. My husband uses the New International Version now, but years ago while building his foundation, he started out with KJV. Here's just a small part of his testimony. I'm sure he won't mind. That's the version that God used to help him learn how to read and to get his CDL license. God told my husband, "If you read your Bible every day before trying to read the CDL book, I'll teach you how to read and retain the information," and of course He kept His word. My husband has been driving a truck (eighteen-wheeler) ever since1994. Okay, let's move on and get back to my testimony.

As I kept the consistency of praying every morning before attending to the husband, kids, etc., my house grew both spiritually and naturally. If you'll notice, I did say "before attending to husband, kids, etc." Well, I do mean just that. It will require you to awaken earlier than the others in the house to get your personal time in with your heavenly Father (make it personal). In the word it does say, "...seek ye first the kingdom of God and all His righteousness; an all other things shall be added unto you. Take therefore no thought for the morrow for the morrow shall take thought for the things of itself. Sufficient unto the day is the evil thereof."

Mathew 6:33-34 KJV. Verse 34 means to keep your mind on Him. Don't worry about tomorrow. You don't have to as long as you put Him first in your day. Worrying about your tomorrow will keep your spirit man in turmoil instead of the peace that God so wants to keep us in each and every day of our lives. I really hope you're a true believer or at least willing to become a true believer of the word of God. Take it for what it says without allowing a doubtful preconceived notion to rob you from what God has in store for your very own personal prayer life. I learned to out of true desperation. I am writing this to you because if you'll truly surrender and you'll truly prosper. God's word does not come back void to Him. It accomplishes that which God pleases and it shall prosper in the thing whereto God sends it (paraphrased). Isaiah 55:11 KJV. That whole chapter speaks about God's promises to us. (I encourage you to read it; this will inspire you.) I am a living testimony that God meets us right where we are. He is not a respecter of persons, especially if you show Him that you're serious about seeking Him first every day, wholeheartedly. Another scripture comes to mind. "Draw nigh to me and I will draw nigh to you." James 4:8 (paraphrased). When we choose to follow God and receive his son as our personal Lord and Savior that makes us the righteousness of God, because we choose to believe without seeing Him with our natural eyesight. That's what made our forefather Abraham RIGHTEOUS. He became the righteousness of God because he chose to believe every word that proceeded from the mouth of God without ever seeing God. He separated himself from his kinfolk because he believed God told him to and so he did it respectfully. I truly believe that when he experienced God speaking to him in his spirit for the first time, it filled that void he had had for so long that could not be filled by worshipping those idols that his father and the rest of his family were worshipping (remember, they could see their idols). Abraham chose to BELIEVE. I cannot convey to you strongly enough how important choosing to believe God at his word is. It will change your life forever. HALLELUJAH!

Chapter Six

Not Settling for Less

Some may say, "Boy, she sure is quoting a lot of scripture." Well, I want you to know none of my victories over any situations in my life like breaking generational curses of kidney failure, homelessness, and divorce came from me. It only came to me from God's awesome word and the Holy Spirit. The Holy Spirit is who made it rhema to me (real). As women and men of faith, we are so involved with family, the ministry, and work, etc., that we can become overwhelmed trying to keep the faith and walk in the spirit at the same time. When this comes, I've found out the following:

#1) I had better stand on the word of God. By doing that, it has to be written on the tablet of our hearts.

#2) I must not look to the left or to the right. I must STAY FOCUSED,

#3) Remember to seek ye first the kingdom of God by praying or spending time with God.

First in my day I set in my heart that I am doing everything for Him and not man. I can guarantee that you will not stay overwhelmed by your situation and circumstances. You will become overwhelmed by the presence of God. I don't know about you, but I can use that type of overwhelming any time, any day, for the rest of my life. This habit will cause fervency and a tenacity to come about your inner man, so much that it will also cause prayer to become a natural spiritual habit for you and your family. I bet you're saying to yourself, "What if I don't get up in time to pray my whole prayer time?" I say the answer to that question is to work very hard at making sure there are no rituals or traditional habits for you to have to spend time with the Father. Please remember these rituals and traditions will always make the word of God have no effect on our lives. Just get up and do what you can. Acknowledge God first and move on through the day. Remember, He is merciful and just and will honor us because He sees our hearts in the matter. He sits high and searches low through the hearts of man. He's awesome like that. I remember trying some rituals/traditions of my sister's in the Lord. They would have to get their Bibles with a cup of coffee and prayer journal. After a few times feeling that I had let God down by not spending enough time and not doing certain things, I began to look at it this way. By the time I did all those steps, I could have already been in his presence. God wants to be our cup of coffee. He wants to write His word on the tablets of our hearts (so we can be a walking Bible). He wants us to be a cup of coffee for others to get them excited and charged up. He also wants to make us a living, walking, prayer journal so we can set the captives free, heal the broken-hearted, and the list goes on, but you get the point. Yes, sometimes it's okay, but we can't let it distract us from our precious time with the Father. I hope I did not offend anyone. That's not my objective while being honest with you. I just don't want anyone to get caught up with what man says and does to get our Heavenly Father's attention or approval. Don't let it affect our REAL Godly understanding of God's unconditional love. You're your own person; there is no one like you. After all, He's just looking for a heart that's ready to serve Him. In the word (Bible) it says: I know the plans I have for you says the Lord plans for a good and not for evil, to give you hope and a future (paraphrased). Jeremiah 29:11.

I would like to convey that you should allow God to write His words on the tablets of your heart. Pray them. Pray them. Pray them. Pray them some more. That's where that old saying: NO prayer NO power SOME prayer SOME power MUCH prayer MUCH power comes in. I like that it speaks for itself, especially praying the word of God. In Hebrews 4:12, it says "...for the word of God is powerful and sharper than any two edged sword piercing even to the dividing asunder of soul and spirit, and of the joints and marrow and is a discerner of the thoughts and intents of the heart." Since the word of God is that powerful all by itself, imagine how powerful it becomes when we pray it and we come into agreement with it by not just reading it but believing it. The word (Bible) will edify your spirit so much that it will become a habit and begin to become spiritual habit to your spirit man. As you grow you will realize that you can't get this anywhere else. Sometimes we'll fall and forget to pray or think we've arrived by not having to press so hard into His presence because we got it going on, but trust this part of my testimony, my sisters and brothers. That's a snare and a lie from the enemy/devil to get you away from your personal connection to God by prayer (our number one tool against him). We are nothing without Him; that's all to it. I have an old saying that I'd like to share with you: There is no grey area, it's black and white and when Jesus spoke, it turned RED! I encourage you, children of the King, don't settle for less. When the bills are due and you don't have the money, PRAY God will make a way out of no way. When there are issues with spouses or children or just life in general, PRAY. Never cease to PRAY God will make a way out of no way. He will give you directions and guidance. He is so faithful that if we don't get it one way He will send you someone like Ignitia, who is one of many that He sent me as my foundation was being built. I am a true living testimony to this. GOD ANSWERS PRAYER.

Always also remember He never leaves us OR forsakes us. I've never found Him to be late on anything. He's always on time. I know there have been trials and tests to keep my faith muscles strong and keep me active in my prayer life. I don't mind because He has never let me down. Things may not go the way we want but if we keep our eyes on Him and trust

Him, we will be able to walk out VICTORIOUSLY. We just have to keep fighting the good fight of faith "…lay hold onto eternal life, whereunto thou art called, and hast professed a good profession before many witnesses…." 1st Timothy 6:12 KJV. Making God our first priority in the day is a guarantee we can't go wrong, but always remember, even if we do, He is so faithful and just to get us back on the right track.

Chapter Seven

Lining Up Some Things

We have to remember first God and then our spouses and then the children. With this order, you will be able to conquer all of life's duties with JOY that's unspeakable that He so graciously allows to flood our souls. If you are single and have your salvation, you have it even better in some ways. Your only obstacle that can throw you off is yourself. If you're not married yet or widowed, REMEMBER to put God first. This applies to anyone in the Kingdom who would like to be prosperous in the natural realm and in the spiritual realm of life. The word in 1st Corinthians 14:40 says "...let all things be done decent and in order." What about me? Well, we have to remember that when we seek God's face first and foremost, we will find Him and in finding Him, He releases His grace which is sufficient for everything throughout any day. Amen. Let's also remember the scripture that I mentioned earlier in our reading. The Bible is a manual for human life to show us how to live (not just exist) and to do things with God's blessing and in His perfect will. So let's keep our eyes on Him and do our best not to allow ourselves to settle for less. We are children of the King, the one, true, only God, and He has given us the authority to trample on serpents and scorpions and over all the power of the enemy/devil. Nothing by any means shall hurt you. Luke 10:19 KJV. This is one of those scriptures that turned RED. AMEN!

Chapter Eight

Today's Testimony on a Lifestyle of Prayer

The word of God says we overcome the enemy/devil by the blood of the Lamb and the word of our testimony. Well, my today testimony is that I've grown and if you think I was growing in confidence in my prayer life, then you should witness my confidence about prayer now. You should see how far God has brought me in my lifestyle of prayer. I have victory in my life—period. I have had so many people that God has sent to help with their prayer teams and their personal prayer lives that took my zealousness about prayer in a general state and not a literal state. Some even mocked me. It hurt me at the time BUT GOD (every now and then I just like to hear those two words—try it—BUT GOD!) is so faithful to heal, restore and give us a double portion for our suffering, especially when we submit and go ahead through the persecution. Then there were and still are those who allowed God to use me in their lives, and they seriously prospered spiritually/naturally from it. There is nothing that I WON'T TAKE TO God in prayer, anyplace, anytime, anywhere. I give God all the glory. I shared this earlier, but I feel the need to share it again—He (God) is the only true father I've ever known outside of Papa John Franklin Owens.

We need to remember a lot of warfare will come our way when we step up to do the things of God but remember this scripture: "Ye are of God, little children and have overcome them: because greater is he who is in you then he that's in the world." 1st John 4:4. We always have to remember that the enemy/devil will try to come after our prayer times because he knows he can't touch you when you're behind the veil with God in prayer. There's another scripture I want to share. Does that surprise you? In sharing this scripture I'm going to share some revelation. I hope you don't mind. It will bless you and you'll never forget it. Psalm 42:1 NIV: "As the deer pants for streams of water my soul pants for thee O'God." The interpretation for this verse is that the deer goes to the stream for safety and to hide its scent from his enemies. He cannot be sniffed out once he reaches the water. His scent is lost completely. Well, we can use this as a spiritual analogy for prayer. As long as we stay in His presence and pray as best we know, the enemy/devil can't pick up our scent and we can hide in God's presence. When going through a storm, don't look to the left or to the right. Stay focused because God says in his word, "...but thou, o Lord, art a shield for me: my glory, and the lifter of my head." Psalm 3:3 KJV. God is the only one who sees your heart. Don't worry about what man says or thinks. STAY focused and you'll be victorious NO MATTER WHAT the outcome may be because we all want God's will anyway, right? (Smile, that's another book.) Okay, moving on now. I keep my eyesight focused on the Lord, as best I can, and I put Him first the best I can and I pray the best I can during storms and trials and tribulations when they come. When I say the best I can, I mean I am human, and I am the first to admit I am nothing without God. So as I press my way and remember to pray, He hears me NO MATTER WHAT and rescues me. Here's a little more of my testimony. I've been on awesomely anointed prayer teams, a prayer partner for TBN, sent to churches to help the prayer life of the church go deeper. People come to my home for prayer or call or email. Mind you, I am not boasting about me. I'm boasting in God. God is a good God unconditionally. God is a faithful God. God is a sovereign God. Not only that, He's the ONE, true, ONLY living God. He's the one, true lover of our souls if we will let Him.

Chapter Nine

Guaranteed with God

Well, there's not much more to say on how to begin a lifestyle of prayer. God is a God of multiplication and He's so faithful, He will grow you in your own personal prayer time and your light will so shine before men, that they may see your good works and glorify your father which is in heaven. Mathew 5:16 KJV. Prayer can only be taught so much and then it has to be caught in our spirit man. Caught means to seize and hold, as after a chase or to seize or take by as a trap, snare etc. (*Webster's* definition). It will then become a spiritual habit and also become the lifeline it's meant to be for us. You will not be able to function in your day without it. It may sound like I'm stretching it a bit, but I'm not really—because you'll actually feel like you can't, due to the fact of the intimate relationship that has formed between you and your Lord God, our maker. He will woo you to remembrance; He does not CONDEMN us to remembrance (like the enemy/devil or even man does). We have to remember that conviction does not feel that great but it's one of the best things we could have for our spiritual growth. Out of our intimate prayer time with Him, He shows our spiritual eyes what our natural eyes can't see. (You'll get so used to knowing what's up BEFORE hand that you won't want to settle for the AFTER.) He fills the voids in our spirit man that formed in our spirits way before we became a confessed child of the King. He causes us to see in the high places so we CAN handle the things in the low places. We CAN overcome every wile of the enemy/devil if we just hide under HIS awesome wing in prayer.

SPECIAL NOTE TO HOUSEWIVES/HOUSEMEN/STAY-AT-HOME PARENTS:

***DO NOT let the enemy/devil oppress you by causing you to feel like you're missing anything. Please know that we all have different walks in life. And we know that all things work together for good to them that love God, to them who are called according to his **purpose**. Romans 8.28 NKJ.

Just be faithful in being that stay-at-home parent because by being faithful in a little, He will make you ruler over much. Our home is our first ministry. God is so faithful that He will raise you up in His timing NO MATTER WHAT man says! Look at me. I'm writing a book and I have at least one at home ready to be finished and edited. So look for it to be out soon. It won't be such an easy read, though.

Here are the scriptures I provided for you in this reading. All of them are from the New King James Version of the Bible with the exception of Psalm 42:1, where I used NIV. I was able to bring better Godly understanding to what I was trying to convey:

(Old Testament)

Jeremiah 29:11

Proverbs 16:17

Isaiah 55:11

Psalm 3:3

Psalm 42:1 NIV

(New Testament)

1st Corinthians 1:27

1st Corinthians 3:7

1st Corinthians 14:40

2nd Corinthians 3:17

2nd Corinthians 5:7

2nd Corinthians 5:17

Mark 8:33

Mark 4:7

Mark 4:39

1st John 4:4

Mathew 5:16

Mathew 6:33-34

Luke 10:19

Ephesians 6:12

2nd Timothy 1:7

1st Timothy 6:12

James 4:7

Romans 8:28

May God bless you, my brothers and sisters in Christ. Use this as a tool. Search out the scriptures I've provided in this book and let God take those scriptures which are logos (written words) and make the rhema (revelation) to your spirit man so you can make a difference in this world through prayer and especially for the building of the Kingdom of God. We need you NO MATTER WHAT! Always remember someone is on the other side waiting for our obedience.

With His love and mine, and staying on the wall of prayer as best I know how, NO MATTER WHAT!

Printed in the United States
114361LV00003B/233/P